I0797670

Dirty Work

DIRTY INDUSTRIAL JOBS

Kenny Abdo

Fly!
An Imprint of Abdo Zoom
abdobooks.com

abdobooks.com

Published by Abdo Zoom, a division of ABDO, P.O. Box 398166, Minneapolis, Minnesota 55439.

Printed in the United States of America, North Mankato, Minnesota.
052025
092025

Photo Credits: Alamy, AP Images, Getty Images, Shutterstock
Production Contributors: Kenny Abdo, Jennie Forsberg, Grace Hansen
Design Contributors: Candice Keimig, Neil Klinepier, Colleen McLaren

Library of Congress Control Number: 2024947686

Publisher's Cataloging-in-Publication Data

Names: Abdo, Kenny, author.
Title: Dirty industrial jobs / by Kenny Abdo
Description: Minneapolis, Minnesota : Abdo Zoom, 2026 | Series: Dirty work | Includes online resources and index.
Identifiers: ISBN 9781098288730 (lib. bdg.) | ISBN 9781098289430 (ebook) | ISBN 9781098289782 (Read-to-me ebook)
Subjects: LCSH: Sanitation--Juvenile literature. | Careers--Juvenile literature. | Factory sanitation--Juvenile literature. | Industrial hygiene--Juvenile literature. | Industrial microbiology--Juvenile literature.
Classification: DDC 331.70--dc23

TABLE OF CONTENTS

DIRTY INDUSTRIAL JOBS

Industrial jobs are challenging and messy, but they support the world we live in. Without them, things would go off the rails quickly!

THE DIRT

Industrial jobs require a lot of physical effort, such as operating heavy machinery in dangerous weather and other conditions. Sometimes, even a small mistake can lead to serious problems, injuries, or even death.

Vocations such as coal **mining**, construction, and steelworking can be dirty but are key in keeping society running. Without them, daily life would grind to a halt!

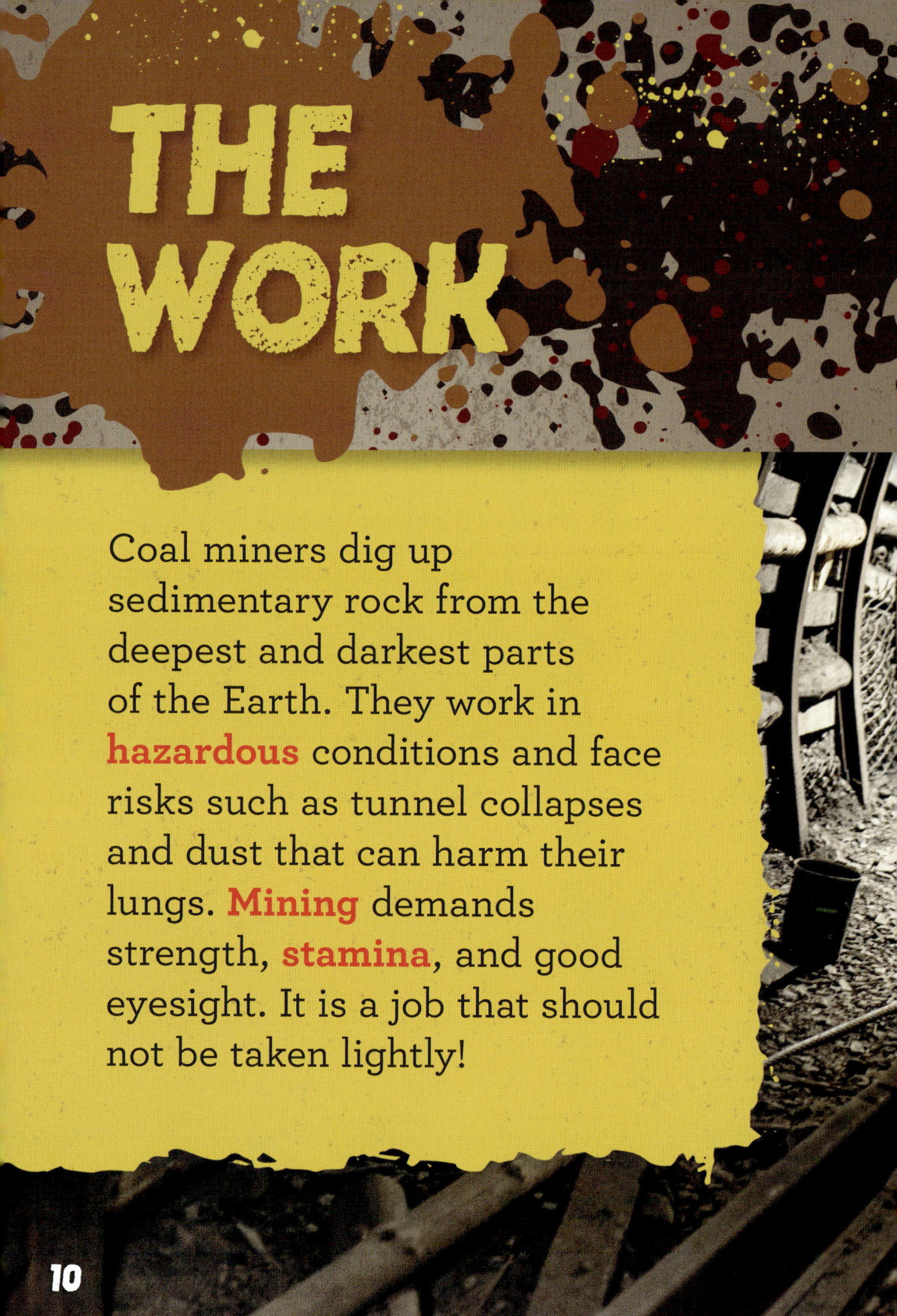

THE WORK

Coal miners dig up sedimentary rock from the deepest and darkest parts of the Earth. They work in **hazardous** conditions and face risks such as tunnel collapses and dust that can harm their lungs. **Mining** demands strength, **stamina**, and good eyesight. It is a job that should not be taken lightly!

Construction crews put in a lot of hard work. They must operate heavy equipment, steer clear of falling objects, and avoid harmful chemicals. Their job is risky but also groundbreaking!

Geoducks are very large saltwater clams. They live on the seabed and are considered a **delicacy**. But how do they go from the ocean to a plate? Geoduck harvesters dive and dig for these treasures in all sorts of dirty and murky conditions!

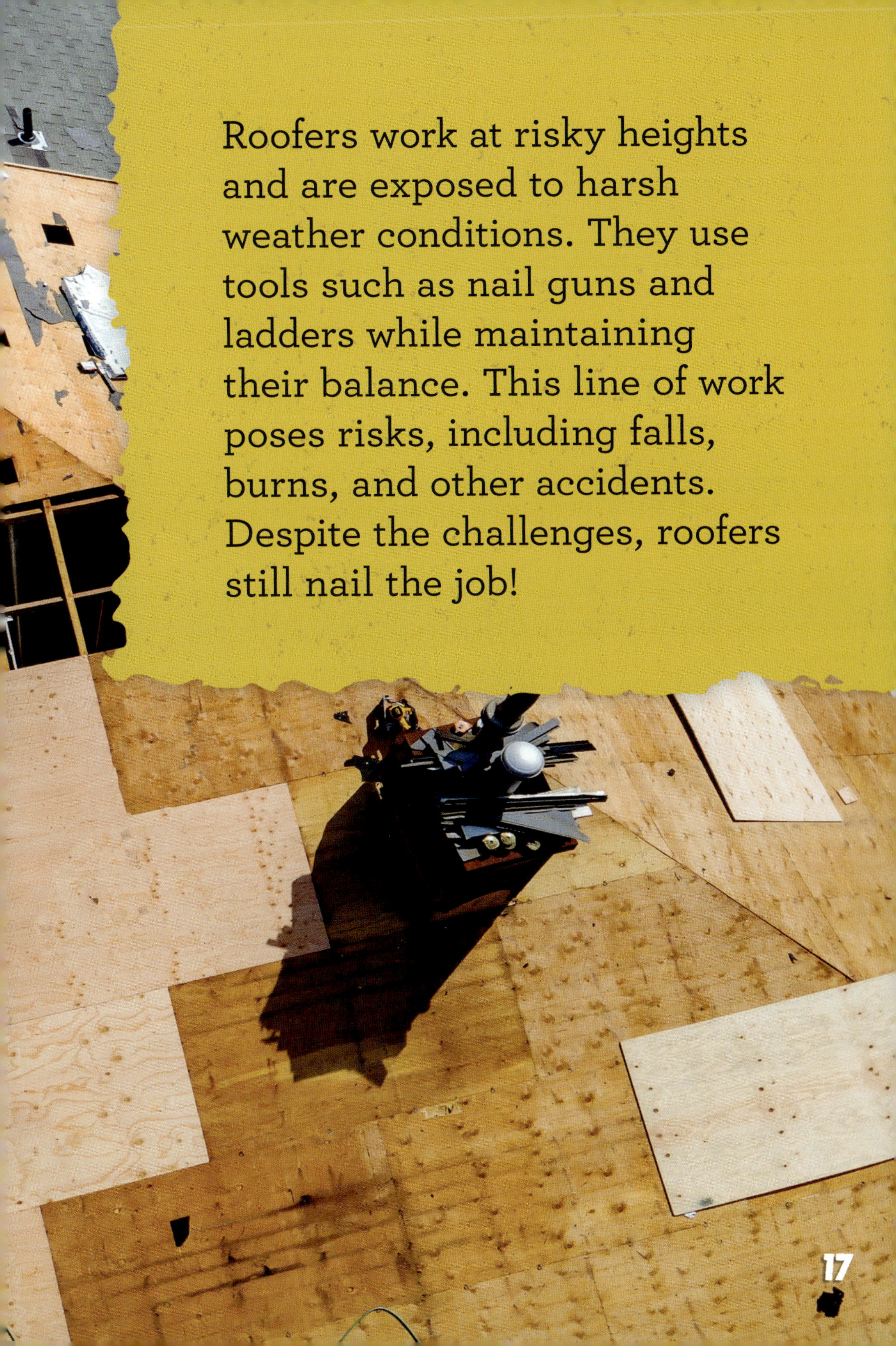

Roofers work at risky heights and are exposed to harsh weather conditions. They use tools such as nail guns and ladders while maintaining their balance. This line of work poses risks, including falls, burns, and other accidents. Despite the challenges, roofers still nail the job!

Steelworkers operate in extreme environments with intense heat. They handle heavy and potentially dangerous materials, such as **molten** metals. The machinery used by steelworkers demands focus. To perform this type of work, one needs nerves of steel!

Railroad maintenance workers are responsible for repairing the tracks and equipment that trains rely on, often in remote areas. Whether it's hot or freezing cold, the crew still operates. Without regular maintenance, the mode of transportation would go off the rails!

Tunnel diggers create underground passages by chiseling and blasting through rock and soil. They work in tight spaces with limited airflow, often covered in mud and dust. Their work is essential for constructing subways and sewer systems. That's something everyone can really dig!

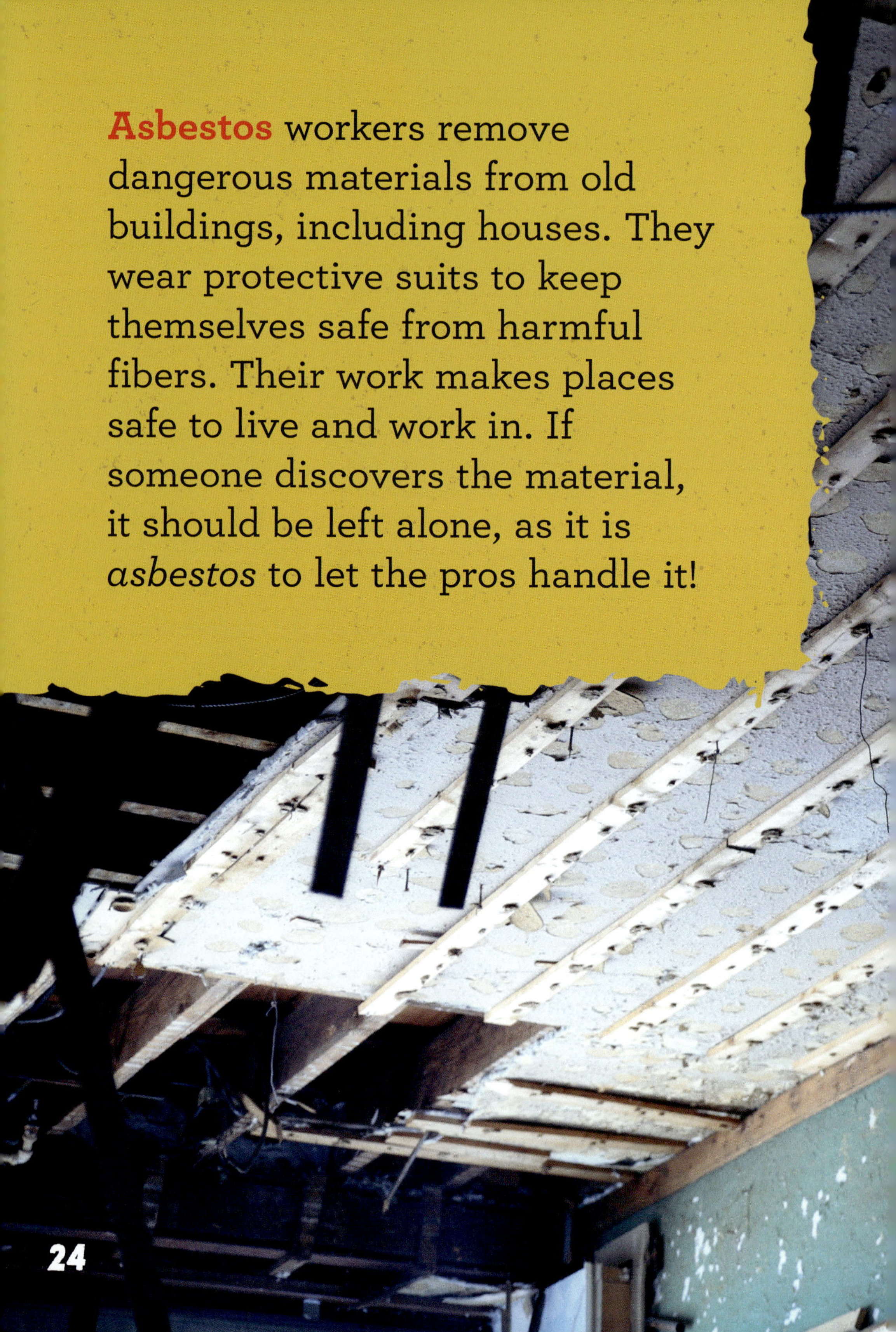

Asbestos workers remove dangerous materials from old buildings, including houses. They wear protective suits to keep themselves safe from harmful fibers. Their work makes places safe to live and work in. If someone discovers the material, it should be left alone, as it is *asbestos* to let the pros handle it!

THE CLEAN UP

Renewable energy **engineers** create systems that use clean energy. They help fight climate change and work toward a healthier planet for future generations. In 2022, renewable energy sources provided over 30% of the world's electricity. This shift is important for building a more **sustainable** future.

These important industrial jobs keep everything from construction sites to trains running smoothly. The workers who take them on really *steel* the show!

GLOSSARY

asbestos – a heat-resistant mineral that can be woven into fabrics. It was often used in fireproof products, like home insulation. It is no longer used because it can cause serious illness, including cancer.

delicacy – a food item that is considered delicious and rare.

engineer – a person who creates or builds structures and devices using science and math.

hazardous – full of danger or having many risks.

mining – the process of obtaining useful materials, such as coal and iron, from the earth.

molten – made liquid by very high heat.

stamina – the strength to handle long effort.

sustainable – of or related to a method of managing or using a resource so that the resource is never used up.

vocation – a person's employment or trade that requires a great amount of dedication and worthiness.

ONLINE RESOURCES

Booklinks
NONFICTION NETWORK
FREE! ONLINE NONFICTION RESOURCES

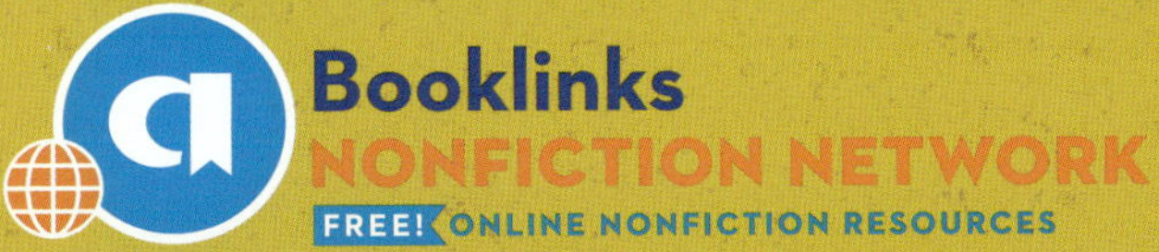

To learn more about industrial jobs, please visit **abdobooklinks.com** or scan this QR code. These links are routinely monitored and updated to provide the most current information available.

INDEX